W9-CME-314

Leatherback Sea Turtle Migration

by Kari Schuetz

BLASTOFF! READERS
3

BELLWETHER MEDIA · MINNEAPOLIS, MN

Note to Librarians, Teachers, and Parents:

Blastoff! Readers are carefully developed by literacy experts and combine standards-based content with developmentally appropriate text.

Level 1 provides the most support through repetition of high-frequency words, light text, predictable sentence patterns, and strong visual support.

Level 2 offers early readers a bit more challenge through varied simple sentences, increased text load, and less repetition of high-frequency words.

Level 3 advances early-fluent readers toward fluency through increased text and concept load, less reliance on visuals, longer sentences, and more literary language.

Level 4 builds reading stamina by providing more text per page, increased use of punctuation, greater variation in sentence patterns, and increasingly challenging vocabulary.

Level 5 encourages children to move from "learning to read" to "reading to learn" by providing even more text, varied writing styles, and less familiar topics.

Whichever book is right for your reader, Blastoff! Readers are the perfect books to build confidence and encourage a love of reading that will last a lifetime!

This edition first published in 2019 by Bellwether Media, Inc.

No part of this publication may be reproduced in whole or in part without written permission of the publisher. For information regarding permission, write to Bellwether Media, Inc., Attention: Permissions Department, 6012 Blue Circle Drive, Minnetonka, MN 55343.

Library of Congress Cataloging-in-Publication Data

Names: Schuetz, Kari, author.
Title: Leatherback Sea Turtle Migration / by Kari Schuetz.
Description: Minneapolis, MN : Bellwether Media, Inc., 2019. | Series:
   Blastoff! Readers. Animals on the Move | Audience: Age 5-8. | Audience:
   Grade K to 3. | Includes bibliographical references and index.
Identifiers: LCCN 2017061809 (print) | LCCN 2018005324 (ebook) |
   ISBN 9781626178175 (hardcover : alk. paper) | ISBN 9781681035581 (ebook)
Subjects: LCSH: Leatherback turtle--Migration--Juvenile literature.
Classification: LCC QL666.C546 (ebook) | LCC QL666.C546 S38 2019 (print) | DDC 597.92/89--dc23
LC record available at https://lccn.loc.gov/2017061809

Editor: Paige V. Polinsky   Designer: Jeffrey Kollock

Printed in the United States of America, North Mankato, MN

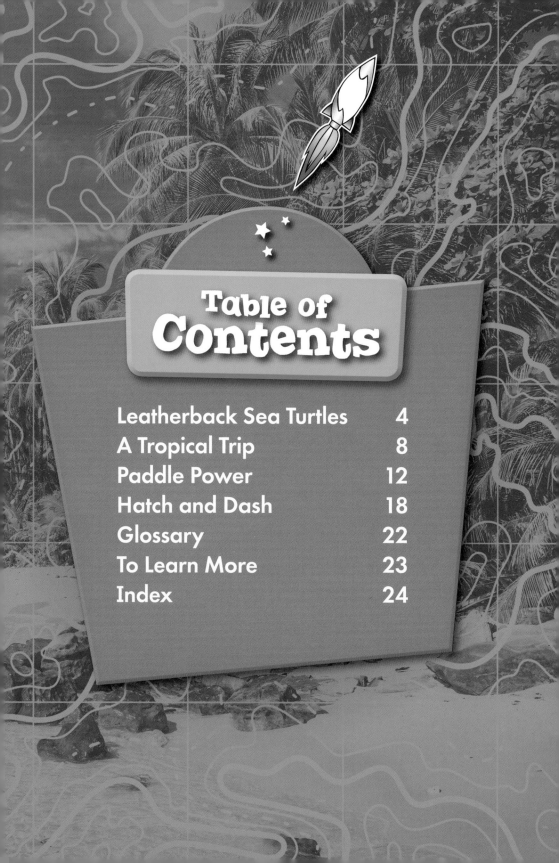

Table of Contents

Leatherback Sea Turtles

Leatherback sea turtles are well-traveled **reptiles**. They live in oceans all over the world.

Leatherback Sea Turtle Profile

animal type: reptile

habitats: oceans, tropical beaches

size: body length: up to 7 feet (2.1 meters)
weight: up to 2,000 pounds (907.2 kilograms)

life span: up to 50 years

Leatherbacks **migrate** farther than any other reptiles. Western Pacific leatherbacks can swim 10,000 miles (16,093 kilometers) a year!

flipper

Leatherbacks use long, winglike **flippers** to fly through the ocean. Their teardrop-shaped bodies cut through water gracefully.

The turtles also have rubbery shells. This gives them **flexibility** when diving deep.

shell

A Tropical Trip

In fall, leatherbacks notice days grow darker. Pink spots on their heads might sense the change in sunlight.

Winter will make food harder to find. The turtles must seek warmer waters. It is nesting time!

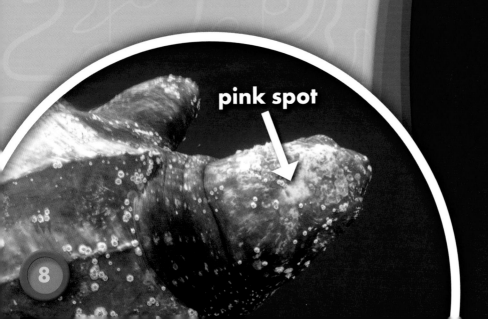

pink spot

Western Pacific Leatherback Departure

mode of travel: swimming

leaving fall: Eastern Pacific coast

arriving winter: Western Pacific beaches

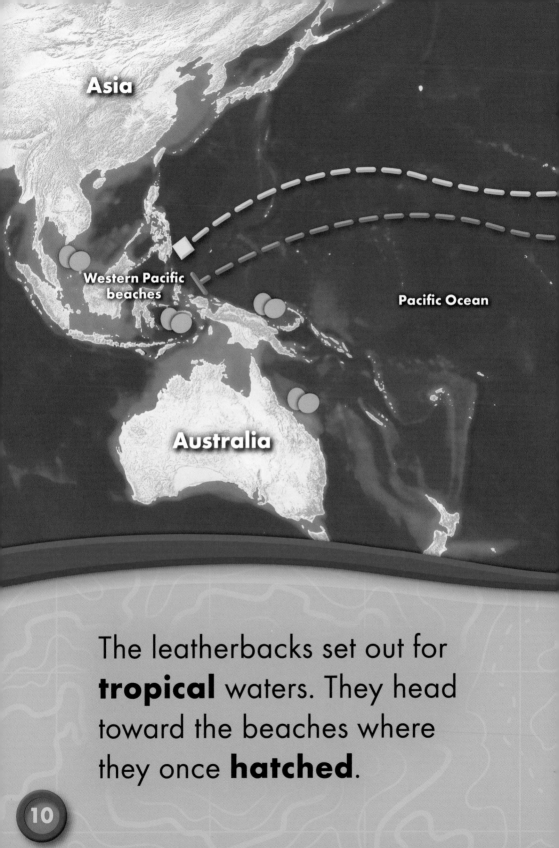

Asia

Western Pacific
beaches

Pacific Ocean

Australia

The leatherbacks set out for
tropical waters. They head
toward the beaches where
they once **hatched**.

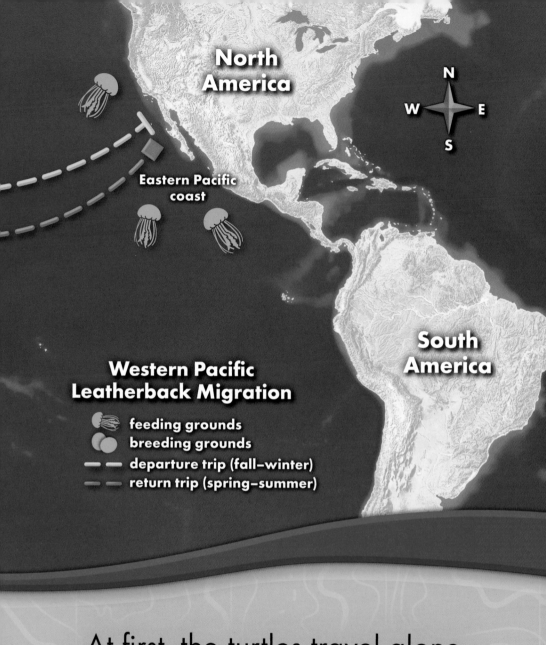

North
America

N
W   E
S

Eastern Pacific
coast

South
America

Western Pacific
Leatherback Migration

- feeding grounds
- breeding grounds
- — — departure trip (fall–winter)
- — — return trip (spring–summer)

At first, the turtles travel alone.
Males and females will later
meet to **breed**.

Paddle Power

Leatherbacks use their front flippers to **propel**. Their back flippers **steer**. Sometimes they ride ocean **currents** to save energy.

Western Pacific Leatherback Dashboard

speed: up to 22 mph (35 km/h)

mph = miles per hour km/h = kilometers per hour

miles traveled per year:

1	0	0	0	0

(16,093 kilometers)

most miles traveled per day:

-	-	-	4	0

(65 kilometers)

Along the way, leatherbacks must surface for air. The turtles cannot breathe underwater.

Leatherbacks must swim with care. Fishing nets can trap them underwater.

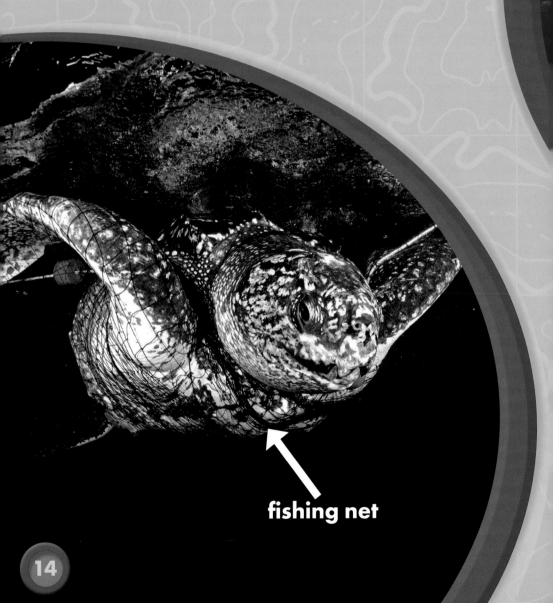

fishing net

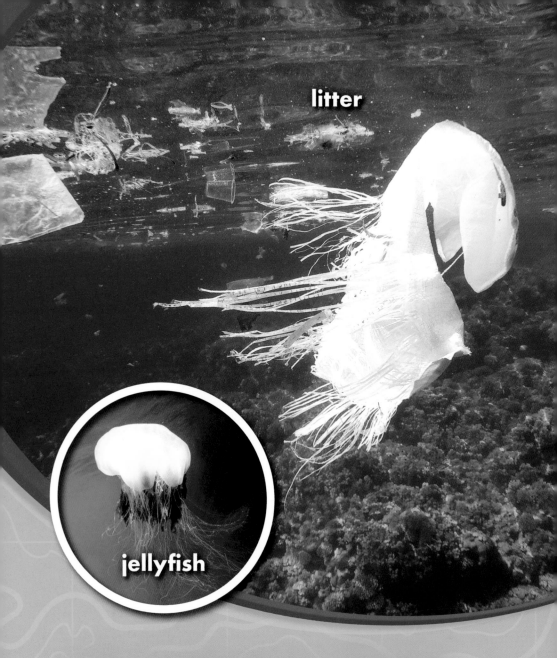

litter

jellyfish

Litter is a threat, too. Floating bags can look like tasty jellyfish. But eating them makes the turtles sick.

Lucky female turtles make it to shore. They dig holes and lay eggs in the sand. About one hundred eggs fill each hole.

This happens several nights during nesting season. Then, they swim back to feeding areas.

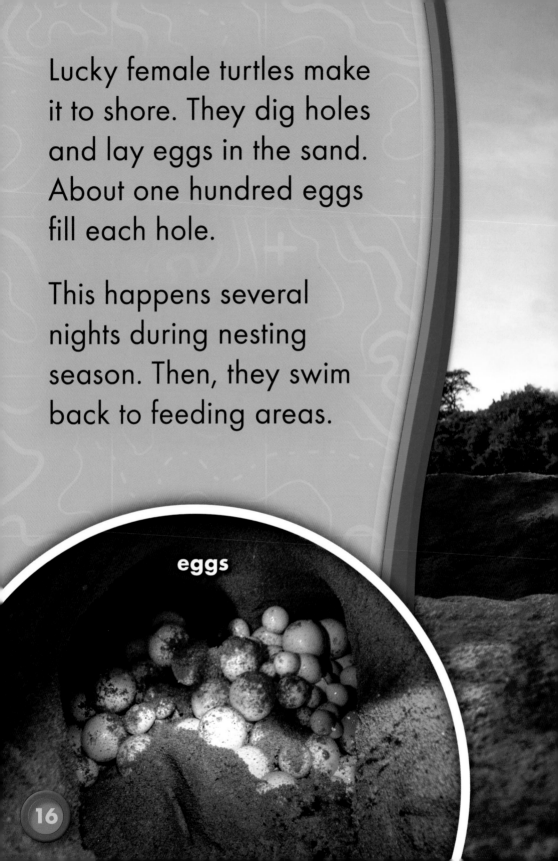

eggs

Western Pacific Leatherback Return

mode of travel: swimming

leaving spring: Western Pacific beaches

arriving summer: Eastern Pacific coast

Hatch and Dash

hatchlings

Hatchlings struggle to survive on their own. **Predators** like crabs attack them as they race toward water.

At sea, many hatchlings become meals for fish and birds.

Young leatherbacks wander the ocean. They spend these years eating and growing.

As adults, they will swim great
distances like their parents.
But first they must grow big
and strong!

Glossary

breed—to produce babies

currents—continuously moving water

flexibility—the ability to bend the body in different ways

flippers—the limbs leatherback sea turtles have for swimming

hatched—broke out of an egg

hatchlings—baby leatherback sea turtles

migrate—to travel from one place to another, often with the seasons

predators—animals that hunt other animals for food

propel—to push forward

reptiles—cold-blooded animals that have backbones and lay eggs

steer—to control direction

tropical—related to the tropics; the tropics is a hot region near the equator.

To Learn More

AT THE LIBRARY

Best, B.J. *Sea Turtles*. New York, N.Y.: Cavendish Square Publishing, 2017.

Hansen, Grace. *Leatherback Turtle Migration*. Minneapolis, Minn.: ABDO Kids, 2017.

Lawrence, Ellen. *A Sea Turtle's Life*. New York, N.Y.: Bearport Publishing, 2017.

ON THE WEB

Learning more about leatherback sea turtle migration is as easy as 1, 2, 3.

1. Go to www.factsurfer.com.

2. Enter "leatherback sea turtle migration" into the search box.

3. Click the "Surf" button and you will see a list of related web sites.

With factsurfer.com, finding more information is just a click away.

Index

The images in this book are reproduced through the courtesy of: Michael Patrick O'Neill/ Alamy, front cover (turtle), p. 9; Elenamiv, front cover (sky); Willyam Bradberry (water/wave); Pla2na, front cover, (gradient map); Doug Perrine/ Minden Pictures/ SuperStock, pp. 4-5; Scubazoo/ SuperStock, p. 5; ACEgan, p. 6; National Geographic Creative/ Alamy, pp. 7, 14, 21; Scubazoo/ Alamy, p. 8; Carefordolphins/ Alamy, p. 12; olenalavrova, p. 15 (top); Joost van Uffelen, p. 15 (bottom); BRUSINI Aurélien/ hemis.fr/ Hemis/ SuperStock, p. 16; Hemis/ Alamy, pp. 16-17; Scottamassey, p. 18; Nature Picture Library/ Alamy, p. 19; Minden Pictures/ SuperStock, p. 20.